Wonder Of Creation
The Natural World Illustrated

Written By
Laura Bowden

Illustrated By
Calvin Leigh Bowden

Wonder Of Creation

The Natural World
Illustrated

Copyright © 2023 Laura Bowden
All rights reserved.

No part of this publication may be reproduced, distributed, or transmitted in any form or by any means, including photocopying, recording, or other electronic or mechanical methods, without the prior written permission of the publisher, except in the case of brief quotations embodied in critical reviews and certain other noncommercial uses permitted by copyright law.

ISBN: 978-0-6397-8768-8

First Edition: Month: 10 May and Year: 2023 of Publication

Cover art by Calvin Leigh Bowden

Illustrations by Calvin Leigh Bowden

"What is this life if, full of care, We have no time to stand and stare."

- W.H. Davies -

God our Lord, is enormous
and impressive!
He is dressed in light
as if it were a huge shiny coat.
He made the sky cover the Earth
like a big tent.

God made the world strong and steady.
It won't ever fall apart.
The Lord wants us to enjoy his creation.
He does fun things.
He rides on soft clouds,
telling the wind to move them along.

He can use anything
to bring us messages.
Fire and flames, thunder and wind,
plants or animals, people, and angels,
Holy Spirit and His written word
deliver messages.

God covered the Earth
with deep water like a big blanket.
The water went up to the mountains
and then flowed back down.
He thundered an instruction to the water,
telling it to go down to the valleys.
The water listened and obeyed.

Now we have rivers and streams
that flow between the hills.
Animals such as donkeys,
sheep, and cows
drink from the streams.
The birds in the sky
build nests by the waters.
They sing among the branches.

Our Lord God
makes the rain fall from the sky
to help plants grow.
The earth is filled with the fruit
of His works.
He gives food to all
the creatures on Earth,
including us.

The grass grows for
animals to eat.
Crops and fruit trees grow for
people to enjoy.
He even makes wine, olive oil,
and bread
to make our lives happier.

The trees grow tall and strong.
Birds make their homes
in their branches.
The storks live in tall Cypress trees.
Little animals hide in the
mountain rocks.

God made the sun and the
moon to shine a light.
The sun tells us when it's daytime,
keeps us warm,
and gives us energy.
The moon shows us the night
and keeps track
of the seasons.

All the forest animals come
out to play when it's dark.
The lions hunt for food,
and when morning comes,
they return to their dens to rest.
When the sun comes up men,
women, and children get up.
They work, learn and play
until it is dark and time to sleep.

The sea is so big and deep,
and it's filled with God's creation.
There are tiny fish and giant whales,
all swimming together.
He gives all His creatures what they need,
and they are always thankful.

God does so many wonderful things!
He made everything,
and the Earth
is full of His amazing creations.
We see Him in all of His cosmos,
plant and animal,
light and darkness, seas and rivers.

When God takes life
away, it is sad.
But when He creates new life,
we are filled with joy.
We depend on you,
God, for everything.

May you always be happy with
your creation, God!

www.ingramcontent.com/pod-product-compliance
Lightning Source LLC
Chambersburg PA
CBHW041203290426
44109CB00003B/119